"Philomel"

Designed, edited and produced
by
Philomel Productions Ltd

Translated by **Sophia Kakkavas**

Typeset : **Bob Shah**
Kall-Kwik, South Kensington
London SW7 3LQ

Colour separations : **Pinas Brothers**
Graphic Arts
Athens, Greece

Montage: **Panos Papadopoulos**
EUROPRINT – Petroulakis
Greece

Printed by **EUROPRINT – Petroulakis**
Greece

Bound by **Moutsis – Iliopoulos**
Greece

All rights reserved. No part of this publication may be reproduced, stored in a retrieval system, or transmitted in any form, or by any means, electronic, mechanical, photocopying, recording or otherwise, without the prior permission of the copyright holder.
© Philomel Productions Ltd, 1993

Published in 1993 by Philomel Productions Ltd, Dublin Ireland

Printed and bound in Greece

Second impression January 1996

ISBN 1 898685 01 0

Ange S. Vlachos

"Philomel"
A modern Greek fable

Illustrated
by
Christos Georgiou

PHILOMEL

"Philomel"
The genesis of the story

"**Philomel**" was written in 1943 when its author, **Ange S. Vlachos**, was just 28 years old. At that time, fables and fairy stories were still widely read in Greece. The texts were not simplified versions but literary masterpieces offering endless hours of pleasure to people of all ages.

Parents would recount the stories to their children, who, once their imagination was kindled, would carry on the tradition. Indeed, it is in this manner that myths, stories and fairy tales have been handed down from generation to generation and survived the centuries.

"**Philomel**" was published in the Greek magazine "Nea Hestia" in 1947. A year later, the author's brother, the painter **Paul Vlachos**, illustrated the story. Text and pictures were sent to the U.S.A. in 1949 but the cost made the publication impossible. The drawings and pictures were sold at various exhibitions. Only two remain in his possession, one print of which is included in this edition; the reader is presented then with two different artistic interpretations of the same story.

The reappearance of "**Philomel**" is owing to the course "What is a Story? A Contemporary Approach", given by **Dr. Bronwen Martin** in 1991–92 in association with the Centre for Extra-Mural Studies, Birkbeck College, University of London. The story was translated

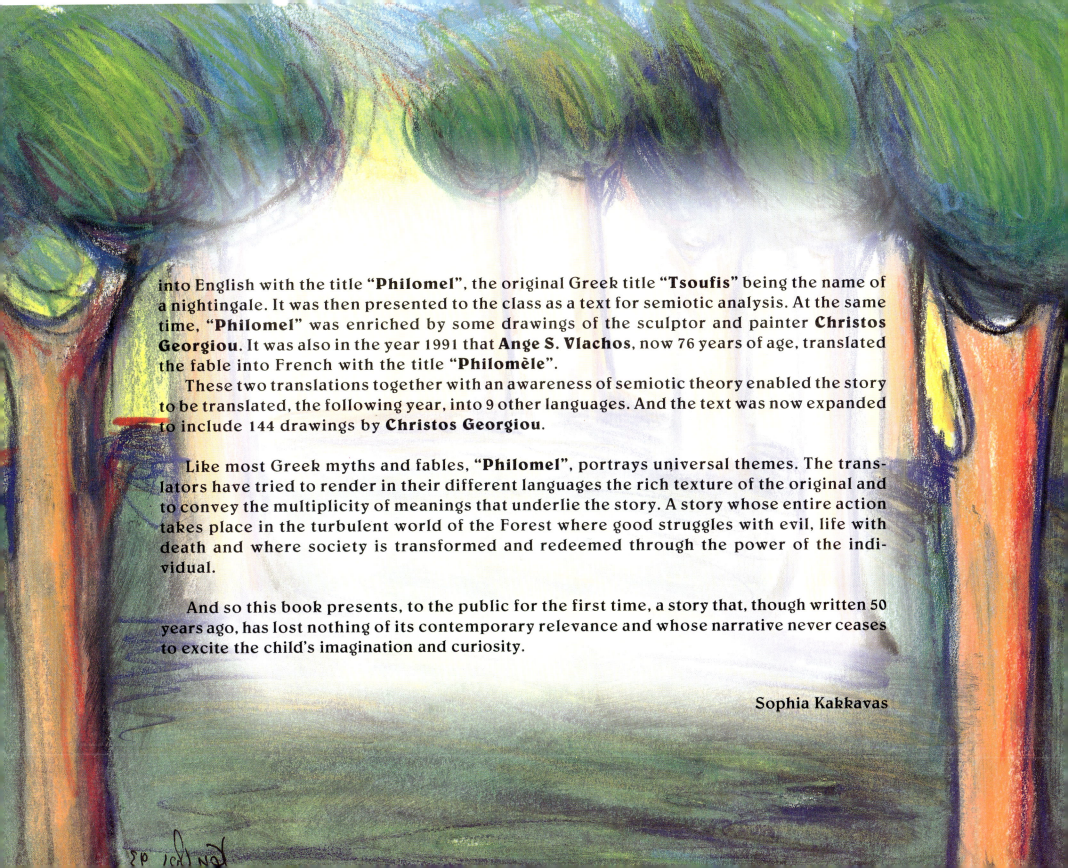

into English with the title **"Philomel"**, the original Greek title **"Tsoufis"** being the name of a nightingale. It was then presented to the class as a text for semiotic analysis. At the same time, **"Philomel"** was enriched by some drawings of the sculptor and painter **Christos Georgiou**. It was also in the year 1991 that **Ange S. Vlachos**, now 76 years of age, translated the fable into French with the title **"Philomèle"**.

These two translations together with an awareness of semiotic theory enabled the story to be translated, the following year, into 9 other languages. And the text was now expanded to include 144 drawings by **Christos Georgiou**.

Like most Greek myths and fables, **"Philomel"**, portrays universal themes. The translators have tried to render in their different languages the rich texture of the original and to convey the multiplicity of meanings that underlie the story. A story whose entire action takes place in the turbulent world of the Forest where good struggles with evil, life with death and where society is transformed and redeemed through the power of the individual.

And so this book presents, to the public for the first time, a story that, though written 50 years ago, has lost nothing of its contemporary relevance and whose narrative never ceases to excite the child's imagination and curiosity.

Sophia Kakkavas

"She will regain her crown only if she kills a Luscinia while it is singing."

"A Luscinia?"

"Hush! ... Hush! ... All of you! Have a little rest now or else you will not hear your father singing."

"Will father sing tonight?"

"Yes he will and the Moon will rise to listen to him. Philomel! Fold your wings! Make room for your brothers!"

"But ... I am too big! What can I do? There isn't room for four ..."

"Be quiet! Don't forget that you were hatched last! Well, this evening, when it is dark, your father will start singing. You must keep quiet. The night will come when you will sing and the Moon will rise to listen ... "

"What is the Moon mother?"

"The Moon is ... oh, well, you'll see the Moon tonight. Hush now, the day is ending, sleep a little. Come closer all of you, closer, under here my children, rest now."

Donna covered her little nightingales with her wings and began a lullaby. Her voice is not as beautiful as her husband's and she knows it.

So she sings only for her children.

And now she is preoccupied with them and disregards the slight crackle. Such a slight crackle like a shrivelled leaf when, stirred by the sigh of the breeze, it rustles over its dead brothers.

A stealthy, creeping sound on the trunk of the linden tree.

"Rest eh!" Chea hissed, "rest for your children! I have a bone to pick with you woman! You're so boastful! You say the Moon rises at your husband's bidding to listen to his chatter all night long! The Moon rises for me! It is for me it wanders, lingering all night! The Moon is looking for me from the sky! But you ... You can not know that!"

Chea uttered her soliloquy, undulating and creeping higher up the tree. She pauses now and then, darting her little head this way, that way.

Like two little pins, her two small eyes penetrate every shadow around her, searching in case someone from the world above, the world of the birds, might see her and alert Donna.

There is also the fear of old Vigo, the Night's Sentinel.

"Hum, him! I must strike him in the daytime.
The accursed one!
I must root him out and exterminate him with my bite.
In the daytime!
He cannot see then!
So tremble my sweet Donna!
I will swallow and devour all the birds of the Forest!"

Chea is a long and dark snake and has a pair of hollow poisonous fangs in her mouth. Night-time or not, her eyes always look menacing.

The birds, the mice, the weasels, even her cousins – the tree-snakes and the water-snakes – avoid her eyes.

All the animals know that if you look into her eyes,
reason takes flight and madness overcomes you.

Chea the Lithe, possesses this power from bygone days, since the days when fairies and goblins used to play in the glades of the Forest by the light of the Moon.

In those days Chea was the daughter of a King,
a daughter of fascinating beauty who wore a crown.

Even now, as a snake, Chea has a circlet on her little head and she boasts that there her crown used to sit.

She maintains that once her mouth is freed of these poisonous fangs, she will regain her long-lost crown.

So in those days Chea used to go dancing, with the other maidens, by the light of the Moon.

And one night, the kind of night that entrances the world and its creatures, when the flowers– narcissuses, crocuses and hyacinths–bewildered stay awake, when even the butterflies do not sleep but fly from blossom to blossom communicating, in the gentlest of whispers, their deepest secrets, on a night like this, when the Forest holds its breath to listen to the song of the Nightingale and, beyond the distant hills, the Moon rises in the sky:

Chea revelled in her dance, tiptoeing on the grass and the flowers, and the Son of Faie saw her for the first time and ... lost his head!

He had looked into her eyes and ...
reason took flight and madness overcame him!

From that moment on, the Son of Faie could think of nothing except to capture Chea. A bush became his hiding place and one night he leapt out and grabbed her.

The frightened maidens, fairies and goblins
flew away from the glades into the woods
and
Chea was left alone with him.

Next came their wedding and the entire Forest celebrated for a month.

I think it was either April or May
when Chea and the Son of Faie were married.

And as everybody partook in merriment and joy forgetting evil thoughts or deeds, the Night's Sentinel had nothing to guard.

Vigo was off duty for the whole month!

Down in the Marshes, amongst the reeds, the Frogs have their Kingdom. They croak all night defending it from the other animals. Defend what! Muddy waters and rotten leaves! Oh well! It is their Kingdom.

Down in these Marshes, there lived an Ogre, they say, but actually what they say is Runa's gossiping, Runa, the magpie who sits idle, tittle-tattling, all day long.

Anyway, they say that this Ogre had a treasure hidden amongst the reeds of the Marshes and, according to these rumours, the Ogre emerged, one day, from the mire, went to the spring, beside the large sycamore, washed and spruced himself and entered the Forest. There the Ogre found Chea surrounded by her bees; they were teaching her the art of making blossom honey.

That day Chea's husband was far away, he had gone to see his mother, the witch Faie. The sight of the Ogre terrified Chea. She had never seen a stranger in the Forest before and the Ogre was so ugly! A real monster! The Ogre talked to Chea in a gentle voice. He told her all about his riches and his jewels and if she would come, he said, into the Marshes, to the Kingdom of the Frogs, he would unearth all his treasures and offer them to her.

"I cannot, I cannot leave the Forest." said Chea, "I must never leave the Forest!"

"Can you imagine how many jewels, how many precious stones I have in the Marshes! It is worth just taking a look at them," the Ogre insisted.

And from that day on,
the Ogre often went to see Chea and, every time,
he promised her his treasures,
if she would only leave the Forest and go with him to the Marshes.

And, one day, as her husband, exhausted from the heat, lay sleeping, Chea left the Forest and went to the Marshes.

As she was about to enter, the wind blew and the reeds around her whispered:
"Where are you going Chea? Where are you going? Go back!"

But the Frogs, who had received their instructions from the Ogre, started to croak:
"Here comes the Queen! She has arrived. The Queen has arrived!"

And Chea entered.

When her husband awoke, he started searching for her.
He asked the birds, he questioned the flowers but no one had anything to tell him.
From high above, Nisoos the hawk, who hovers all day between sky and earth and sees everything that happens in the world, called to him:

"To the Marshes! Go to the Marshes!"

He ran to the Marshes and saw Chea emerging from the muddy waters, filthy from the mire. In the depths, amongst the reeds, he also saw the Ogre who was laughing at him.

Trembling with rage, the Son of Faie, in his fury, called his mother, the Witch. Faie bound Chea's feet, threw her to the ground, snatched her crown, put poison in her mouth and cast a fearful spell on her:

"From now on,
filthy as when you emerged from the mire,
you will crawl on your belly and
whatever you eat from your mouth
will be poisoned."

Chea, rolling on the ground, begged for mercy and Faie, who did not wish to deprive any creature on earth of all hope, told her that only if she killed a bird while it is singing, could she be released from her curse.

The poison would then be discharged from her mouth,
she would become the King's daughter once again,
and rise high into the sky to seek her husband.

Since those far-off days
the King's daughter has become a snake.
Creeping on her belly,
she bites everyone who crosses her path
hoping to get rid of the venom from her fangs but,
in vain.
And Chea's days are filled with despair.

So, creeping up the linden tree, she stopped and her little eyes penetrated the shadows.

She could hear Donna restlessly moving in her nest as if she were frightened by the absolute silence which suddenly falls upon the Forest at this hour. The twilight hour, when the activities and movements of the Day stop and the mysteries of the Night begin.

At this hour even Chea would crawl lazily in the grass looking for a cool place to spend the night.

But this evening, she is out for prey and she must hurry along.
In no time, he will come back, he, the conceited one who sings all night believing that the entire Forest, together with the Moon, listens to him!
If he should return to his nest, then Chea would have to fight with two birds.
And two birds who fight for their children are a peck of trouble, even for Chea.

She crept up, curled her body and fixed her eyes on the nest. At that very moment, a faint whistle was heard, so faint, only a snake's ears could detect it:

"Vigo! The Night's Sentinel! Already awake?"

And Chea slithered down into the darkness.

The Night's Sentinel is the only bird in the Forest
who can see through the darkness.

The stars had come out one by one.
The larger ones first,
in accordance with the order of the sky,
then all the others.

Down below, in the Forest, the Fireflies started to stir.
They used to be stars once, the Fireflies say, that fell to earth.
In spring they shimmer and fly from bush to bush.

They assume the time will come for them to ascend, once again, to where they belong, high in the sky. They say one night without malice in the Forest would suffice, then they would rise high ...

Suddenly,
in the profound silence of the Forest,
the song of the Nightingale was heard.

The wild violets who whisper when the light of the day ends and every fragrant whisper from them perfumes the air, yearned for the song in the half light; the little owl who every now and then stops his solitary chatter and pricks up an ear, longed to hear it; even the silent stream which flows so calmly as if it has stopped, craved for the song to begin.

And higher than the trees escalated the voice of the Nightingale, scale by scale it was raised to be heard in the heavens.

And as the entire Forest listened to the song which floated with the Night,
little by little,
beyond the distant hills,
rose the Moon.

"The Nightingale has lost its reason! He is mad!" the little owl was crying.
And the wild violets, low, in the grass, whispered:
"If only the same could happen to us ..."

To learn how to fly is not an easy task even if you are a bird.

Donna returned, one day, to her nest and found her sons jumping about and flapping their wings. The time had arrived for them to fly. And soon Vigo would come to teach them about the world.

One afternoon, when the sun sits in the middle of the sky and all living creatures, exhausted from the heat, look for shade, Donna placed Philomel on the rim of the nest and told him to look down at Zeena, the may-beetle, who was buzzing in a patch of light like those the sun makes through the leaves.

Zeena was playing with the light and the light with her and Philomel craned further and further to take a closer look at their game.

It was then that Donna nudged him gently out of the nest and,
it happened:

Philomel stretched out his wings and slowly glided to the ground, close to the place where Zeena was playing. Donna flew after him to protect him. Philomel, adventurous, felt immense joy at the abundance of space and started to strut about.

He began to flap his wings and to chirp noisily with delight.

Donna, worried the noise might awaken an enemy, scolded Philomel to quieten him down but Philomel would not comply.

A voice was heard from above, saying:
"I have never seen such a brave little nightingale before!",
Philomel raised his head to see who was talking. It was Lady Squirrel who, high up, on a bough, was looking at him with deceitful eyes.

Lady Squirrel is a peculiar animal. While she is chewing a hazel-nut or something similar, she sits on her hind legs, joins her front little paws, thanking the Lord who feeds her.

Hypocrisy, no doubt!

She is the only one who claims to be praying and the only one who believes it!

Donna was startled at Lady Squirrel's voice. This crafty Lady, who jumps from bough to bough as if she has a spring inside her and she has four legs – did you hear? four ! – this lady, when playing, sometimes gives scratches that can kill!

"Bless the little Nightingale! Bless you! You've sent him into the world too soon, Madame." And Lady Squirrel started to come down from the boughs to the trunk and from the trunk to reach the ground at such speed that Philomel had scarcely time to fly onto a low branch and from there to another one higher until he arrived at his nest. From there he shouted at the top of his voice:

"You are a wicked animal!"

Philomel caused the utmost confusion to his slumbering brothers:

"What on earth is going on? What is the matter with you, Philomel?"

"I came across Danger!"

"What is that? Danger? What does it look like?"
All his brothers wanted to know.
And as a true expert, Philomel announced:

"Danger has four legs!"

"Four legs! How's that?"

"Danger has many legs," said mother Donna,
"so many,
they cannot be counted."

So Philomel had started to learn about the ways of the world.
For other, more serious, matters,
Vigo came to teach him.
Vigo explained briefly to Philomel the constitution of the Forest.

Philomel learned that in the Forest exist two worlds:
the one below and the one above.

He learned that the first tries constantly to do its utmost to harm the second.
He also learned that the weasels, martens, foxes and ferrets as well as all the other creatures that run and jump in the world below, apart from the Hare, constitute a living Danger.
Vigo gave him advice on nutrition: grasshoppers, spiders and insects of all kinds promote growth, he said, but he warned Philomel never to pick up filthy worms.
They come from a lower world,
a muddy and dirty one.
They are distant relatives of Chea, the frightful snake ...

And at this point, Philomel's mind began to wander. He was trying to imagine that peculiar creature and how you could lose your reason by looking into her eyes.

"Has Chea beautiful eyes?" asked Philomel.

"No! No! They are dull and evil, all creatures have clear eyes, only hers ... ", said the wise old Bird and shuddered as if he had remembered something from the days of his youth ...

"And has she no mercy for anyone?"

"Mercy? One must have a heart to have mercy. Chea has no heart since the day she was cursed. Sometimes though, when your father sings in the night, she lingers, wandering like the Moon. Something from her past, when she used to dance with the fairies, must remain in her."

"Vigo, do you remember Chea when she was the King's daughter?"

"It is a very old story. My grandfather, to whom the story was told by his grandfather who had heard it from others, recounted it to me!"

"And will she ever be the King's daughter again?"

"They say she will regain her crown only if she kills a Luscinia while it is singing."

"A Luscinia? What is a Luscinia, Vigo?"

"A bird, a songbird ... Killing a songbird while it is singing! That's impossible!"

Vigo flew back to his lofty abode and left Philomel alone.

Philomel remained on the branch of the linden tree and searched for Chea over the floor of the world below. He recalled Vigo's words:

"Never look into her eyes, never!"

But Philomel had to see her.

He wanted to see what she looked like ... this daughter of a King.

The Days passed and the Nights followed, changing nothing in the Forest, except that Philomel, nightingale that he was, had taught himself how to sing.

His voice was so sweet
and he could sing such beautiful songs,
that even the crickets ceased their unendurable nocturnal chatter
to listen to him.

The more Philomel grew and the more he sang, the more confident he became and he started flying closer to the world below the trees, into low-spreading branches and bushes, observing every kind of activity.

The ants became his friends, he never harmed them.

They used to stop in their path to talk to him about their hard work, to explain how heavily laden they were all day long and how tired they became by the end of the day.

They wondered why Philomel had condescended to listen to them. So they advised him to be vigilant because, in the world below the high trees, over the floor of the Forest, there are many vicious enemies.

Only the Hare harms no one.

Philomel flew in search of the Hare.

He found him nibbling and chewing. He was moving his lips up and down as if the tender, bursting shoots disgusted him.

The Hare heard the flapping of Philomel's wings and flattened his long ears back, crouching on the ground.

"Don't be scared!" called Philomel and landed on a branch nearby.

"Oh! It's you!" sighed the Hare with relief, "you frightened me out of my wits!"

"Do Hares have wits?" Philomel teased him.

"I am a docile, humble animal," said the Hare. "I do not harm anybody."

"I know that! Vigo and the ants told me! So, what's it like to live down here?"

"To live here? We live with fear in our hearts and we lose heart from fear."

"Are you all afraid?"

"Of course we are! Didn't you know that? The marten is afraid of the weasel, the weasel is afraid of the ferret, the ferret is afraid of the fox and the fox is afraid of the wolf. Everyone is trained by fear down here and everybody dreads Chea. As for myself, I fear them all, including Chea – and my shadow."

"You're so harebrained and such a coward!" cried Philomel and flew away.

But, by now, Philomel had learned
about the circle of fear
that binds all creatures to the same fate.

The Days were passing by and, along with them, Summer.
It was nearing the time when trees, tired of holding their leaves, slowly begin to shed them onto the ground, yellow and faded.

Autumn was approaching.

One morning, Donna heard a honking noise from the sky.

She looked through the canopy of the linden tree. High up, in the azure of the sky, she saw the familiar V-shape: the geese!

"We must get ready!"

She started giving instructions to Philomel and his brothers, preparing them for the long journey they were about to take.

And it was at that crucial moment that
Philomel said to his mother
that he wanted to see Chea.

Donna's heart leapt into her mouth!

"Have you taken leave of your senses Philomel? You have grown up and become a real nightingale, but where are your brains? Imagine wanting to see Chea! You've lost your mind before even seeing her!"

"Mother, if I meet Chea and sing to her she might get rid of the poison in her mouth and become the King's daughter once again. And so, the world below us will be freed from her evil."

"Philomel! Get it out of your mind!
What does the world below us matter to you?!"

Philomel flew away to seek advice from Vigo.
The sun had not yet set and Vigo was still asleep.

Philomel sat on a branch nearby to wait and then: he saw close, very close to Vigo's tree a long dark creature. It stirred and undulated on the ground.

It is Chea, the bewitched daughter!
She is crawling on her belly.
She is going to bite Vigo!
But it is not yet dark and he cannot see!
He cannot even move!

Philomel flew closer and called out:
"Vigo, be careful, Vigo! Chea is heading for your tree!"
Vigo heard him but did not move.

Philomel began fluttering round Chea. Chea forgot Vigo and turned to Philomel.

"Look at me, you little idiot!
Look into my eyes and stop singing!
You are annoying me!"

But Philomel knew everything and avoided her eyes.
Still singing, he took flight – with Chea in pursuit.

Vigo was left alone.

From his tree-abode he hearkened to the sound of Philomel's wings
and Chea's hissing.

Deep silence.
Stillness in the Forest.
There was only Vigo, impatient and anxious for the sun to set.

And as the light dimmed,
he flew in the same direction he had last heard Philomel and Chea.

Not far from there, on the ground, with wings outstretched,
Philomel lay lifeless and ... next to him ...

"What is it? What is this strange thing?" thought Vigo.

Around Philomel, hosts of his friends, the ants, had gathered. They had heard the bad news and had hurried there to see.

Vigo wept for Philomel and then he looked all around him.
"Where on earth is Chea?" he wondered.

In the first shadows of the Night, the Fireflies provided the answer.

"At last we will rise into the sky!
High up above, where Chea has gone,"

they called to one another.

The Night's Sentinel turned his head to the sky and saw
between the Little and the Great Bear
a line of shining stars which resembled the shape of Chea.

He saw her long body which winds around like a serpent amongst the other stars
and her little head with the two glittering eyes.

Amazed, Vigo lowered his head.
He looked down to the ground:

Philomel lay lifeless and next to him the cast-off skin of Chea!

Not even a sigh was heard in the Forest.

Serenity reigned high in the trees
and higher in the sky.

Peace ...

... had nestled in the world below.

Paul Vlachos, 1947

"Amazed, Vigo lowered his head..."
episode 33, page 138.

The illustration is printed at its actual size of 72 x 75 mm

Ange S. Vlachos

Books

1. *The Witch's Grave* (Albanian Campaign), 1945
2. *My Master Alcibiades* (historical novel), 1953, Ouranis Prize
3. *Hours of Life,* Prize of the Ministry of Education, 1958
   (fiction: a prisoner's life in the German camps during the Occupation)
4. *Their Most Serene Majesties* (historical novel), 1963
5. *Lucky Daimas* (short stories), Prize of the Ministry of Education, 1968
6. *Partialités chez Thucydide* (essay), 1970, in French
7. *Herodotus the Wronged* (essay), 1970
8. *A Philhellene in 1821* (the Greek War of Independence, historical novel)
   Prize of the Academy of Athens, 1972
9. *The 14th of Nizan,* 1972
10. *Pilgrims to Susa* (essay), 1973
11. *Green Moscow,* 1976
12. *Xerxes: Private Papers* (fictional portrait), 1978
13. *Ten Years of Cyprus* (history), 1980
14. *The Ravings of Pythia,* 1983
15. *Once Upon a Time a Diplomat* (memoirs)
    6 Volumes: I 1985 III 1986 V 1987
    II 1985 IV 1986 VI 1988
16. *In Inverted Order* (Prothysteron), 1990
17. *The King's Shadow,* 1991
18. *Tsoufis: A Fable,* 1993
19. *Ecclesiastes,* 1994
20. *Commentaries on Thucydides,* 1994
21. *Lyrical Short Stories,* 1995

Translations

1. Thucydides, *The Peloponnesian War,* 1965, Book I-VIII
2. Herodotus, *The Histories,* 1972, Book I-IX
3. Aeschylus, *Prometheus Bound,* 1973
4. *The Gospels: Matthew, Mark, Luke, John,* 1977
5. A. Camus, *Calligula,* 1978
6. Aristoteles, *The Constitution of Athens,* 1980
7. G.M. Woodhouse, *The Greek War of Independence,* 1980
8. *Cavafy's: Poems,* 1981 (from Greek into French), Silver Medal of the Académie Française
9. *The Acts of the Apostles,* 1985
10. Cavafy, *Inedited Poems* (bilingual edition, Greek/French), 1995

Theatre

1. *The Belfry* (inspired by the life of the Russian architect Kovnir, XVIIth century)
2. *The Failure of a Resurrection* (the clandestine life of a communist during the Franco regime in Spain)
3. *The Sheep Merchant* (the second marriage of Aspasia)

Translated works of the author

1. *The Witch's Grave* (partly in French)
2. *Their Most Serene Majesties* in English, published by Bodley Head, London 1963, the Vanguard Press, New York
3. *My Master Alcibiades,* in Romanian, published by Editura Univers, Bucharest, 1970
4. *Hours of Life* (translated into English by Peter Bien), published by "The Charioteer", New York, 1972
5. *Pilgrims to Sousa,* in Romanian, published by Editura Univers, Bucharest, 1976
6. *Philomel, a modern Greek fable* in English and Irish (original title «Tsoufis: A Fable»), published by Philomel Pros Ltd, 1993
7. *Ecclesiastes* in Irish, Spanish, Scottish-Gaelic, Welsh, French, Catalan, Italian, published by Philomel Productions Ltd, 1995

Ange S. Vlachos

- Born in 1915 in Egypt. Graduated in Law, University of Athens, 1937
- Joined the Greek Diplomatic Corps in 1939

He was appointed to the following posts:

- Vice-Consul to Constantinople
- First Secretary to the Embassy in Rome
- Consul General to Jerusalem and Cyprus
- Permanent Delegate to the U.N.O., Geneva
- Director of Cultural Affairs to the Foreign Ministry
- Ambassador to Moscow
- Secretary General to the Ministry of Foreign Affairs
- Minister to the Prime Minister in the Karamanlis Government, 1974
- Director General of Radio -Television, Greece, 1975 - 76
- Member of the Academy of Athens, 1985

Decorations:

Greek
Grand-Croix du Patriarchat Œcuménique
Grand Officier de l'Ordre de Georges 1er
Grand Officier de l'Ordre du Phoenix
Commandeur de l'Ordre du St. Sépulcre
Médaille Militaire 1940
Médaille Militaire 1943

Foreign
Grand Officier de l'Ordre du Mérite (Yougoslavie)
Grand Officier de l'Ordre de Vladimiresku (Roumanie)
Commandeur de la Légion d'Honneur (France)
Commandeur de l'Ordre du Mérite (Italie)

Christos Georgiou

Individual exhibitions

Paris

Maison des Beaux Arts, 1974

Athens

Ora Cultural Centre, 1975
O Gallery, 1979
dada art gallery, 1983
Antenor Gallery, 1986
Antenor Gallery, 1988
Titanium Gallery, 1993

Group Exhibitions

France

Maison des Beaux Arts, Paris
Grand Palais des Indépendants, Paris
Musée Rodin, Paris

Poland

Greek Engraving Exhibition, Warsaw

Greece

Panhellenic Exhibitions, 1975 – 1988, in Athens
"Engraving Exhibition", National Gallery, Athens
Antenor Gallery
Adyto Gallery
Ora Cultural Centre
Titanium Gallery

Books

Engravings for the book "Ammos" by M. Bourboulis, published by "Diaton"
Engravings for the book "Sienna" by Yolanda Pegli, published by "Diaton"

The illustrations and covers for the books:
"Judas Century" and "The Descent from the Cross" by Th. Anthimos, published by "Aeolos" 1989–1990

Works of Christos have been bought by:
The National Gallery, Athens, Greece and the Vorae Museum, Paeania, Greece

Works of his can be found in private collections in:
England, U.S.A., France and Greece

Christos Georgiou

- Christos was born in Schimatari, Thebes, Greece, 1943
- He studied in Athens and Paris:

Athens

- Graduated from the Doxiades School of Art, 1968
  Teachers: A. Asteriadis, Yiannis Tsarouchis, Tassos, V. Katraki,
        D. Mytaras, D. Dekoulakos, P. Zoumpoulakis

Paris 1969 – 1976

- Received a scholarship for postgraduate studies from the French Government:
  Ecole des Beaux Arts
  a) Atelier de Sculpture, Maîtres: Etienn Martin, Cesar, Collamarini
  b) Atelier de Gravure, Maîtres: Dayese, Legrance
- Won the first prize for sculpture in the 1974 exhibition for scholarship holders
- Founder-member of the Association of Greek Sculpture

Paul S. Vlachos

Paul S. Vlachos
painter

- **Paul S. Vlachos** was born in Mansura, Egypt in 1921
- He graduated from the School of Arts in Athens in 1943 and from 1947-50 he studied stage design at the 'Old Vic Theatre School' in London, U.K.

Individual exhibitions:
Athens (Greece), Nairobi (Kenya), London (U.K.)

- **Group exhibitions:**
Athens, Greece
2 Panhellenic exhibitions in Athens

- Works of Paul S. Vlachos have been bought by the National Gallery, Athens, Greece and works of his can be found in private collections in Greece

- **Books:**
Covers for the books of his brother, Ange S. Vlachos, *Lucky Daïmas*, 1968, *The 14th of Nizan*, 1972
Pilgrims to Susa, 1973, *The Gospels: Matthew, Mark, Luke, John*, 1977

- **Illustrations and covers for the books:**
- *Philomel, a modern Greek fable* (original title *Tsoufis: A Fable*)
    Paul S. Vlachos (at the age of 26) was the first artist whose illustrations fully interpreted the story of *Philomel* written in 1943 by his brother, Ange S. Vlachos. To date only two of these illustrations remain in his possession. Half a century later, one of these two drawings was included in the hardback edition of the story of *Philomel* which –translated into Irish– was published for the first time in 1993 by Philomel Productions Ltd, Dublin, Ireland.

- *Ecclesiastes* (a personal rendering of the original Greek text of *Ecclesiastes* (Chapter III) by his brother, Ange S. Vlachos) in 1993. Published by Philomel Productions Ltd in 1994, in Greece.
    In 1995, Paul S. Vlachos designed the covers for *Ecclesiastes* in 8 languages (Scottish-Gaelic, Irish, Welsh, French, Italian, Spanish, Catalan). His illustrations of the text of the Greek edition were used in all 8 versions. Published by Philomel Productions Ltd, 1995.

- *The Search for Gold: Space and Meaning in J. M. G. Le Clézio*, a critical study of four of Le Clézio's works, by Dr. Bronwen Martin. Published in 1995 by Philomel Productions Ltd, Dublin, Ireland.